Jules Olitski

The Late Paintings

A Celebration

For Jules

We Miss You

Celebrate: Turquoise, 2007, acrylic on canvas, 9 x 12 inches

Jules Olitski

The Late Paintings

A Celebration

NOVEMBER 8, 2007–JANUARY 5, 2008

ESSAY BY NORMAN L. KLEEBLATT

SUSAN AND ELIHU ROSE CHIEF CURATOR, THE JEWISH MUSEUM, NEW YORK

KNOEDLER & COMPANY

— ESTABLISHED 1846 —

19 EAST 70 STREET NEW YORK NEW YORK 10021

TEL 212 794-0550 FAX 212 772-6932

WWW.KNOEDLERGALLERY.COM

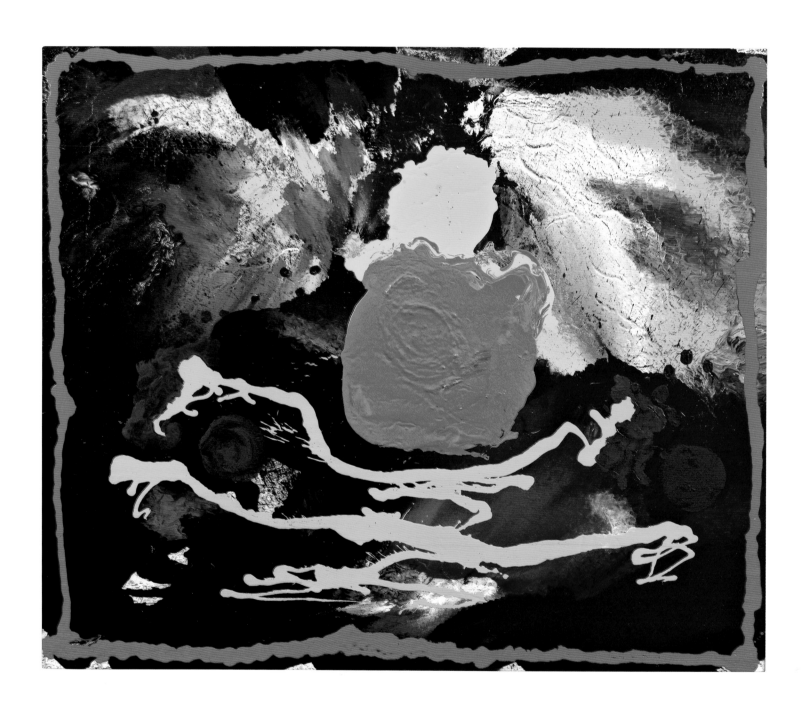

Prince Patutsky Memoir: Turquoise and Yellow, 2004, acrylic on canvas, 59 1/2 x 72 inches

A CULMINATION OF CONTRADICTIONS: JULES OLITSKI'S LAST DECADE

Not quite a year ago I visited a world-famous private collection of postwar American art. The collection included works by major American masters from Jackson Pollock and Willem de Kooning to Elizabeth Murray and Susan Rothenberg; the selections were stellar, each example chosen from the artist's classic period. This usually meant unmistakable signature works that were easy to identify. As my tour neared its end, I was confronted by a luminous abstraction, the work of a painter whom I could not instantly identify (though his identity emerged after I scratched my head for thirty seconds). From medium distance the picture read as a cluster of irregular flagstone-like shapes resembling an outdoor patio that had been tilted upward by ninety degrees. The paint color with its metallic luster was impossible to describe. At first glance the painting seemed *trompe l'oeil.* Yet its three-dimensional allusions incongruously balanced a constant tension with the flatness of the painting's support. Haunting and brash at the same time, it turned out to be an early 1980s piece by Jules Olitski which the discerning collectors recognized as a major work. Given the classic nature of the collection, I would have expected a more canonical Olitski: perhaps a work from the early 1960s featuring his radically reduced nesting shapes with their saturated, high-key and ultra-flat use of color, or even better, a mid-1960s "spray"—the pure, all-over paintings produced by Olitski's revolutionary co-option of the paint sprayer. After all, it was the latter paintings that prompted critic Clement Greenberg to pronounce Jules Olitski heir to Jackson Pollock.

Indeed the writings of formalist critics such as Clement Greenberg and Michael Fried, to name the two best known, have left an indelible mark on future readings of Olitski's later work. Their arguments situated his pictures from the 1960s as part of a well-known, if somewhat narrow canon, blocking Olitski's subsequent achievements from being seen within the wider pluralist practices of the 1970s to now. To further such tightly argued theories, Olitski's ensuing career would oblige an evolutionary theory, the kind of logical progression imposed as linear stylistic development in the careers of, for example, Paul Cézanne and Piet Mondrian. Olitski himself balked at theories about his work. When curator Henry Geldzahler, who in 1969 gave Olitski a one-person show at The Metropolitan Museum of Art, proposed an evolutionary progress for Olitski's paintings, arguing that the work started thick, then became thin in the mid-1960s, then started to thicken up again, the artist objected. Olitski claimed ". . . you can't account beforehand for what happens inside the work while it's being made . . . we don't prepare for art, we make art."[1] Olitski later boasted of having "no theory of color" despite his position as a leader of the Color Field movement.[2]

Yet many writers on Olitski's later work agree that a theoretical, evolutionary reading would be both unfair and impossible to sustain. Olitski's post-1960s art remains too far-ranging, too varied, too experimental, too vast in its deployment of sources, and simply too playful to be sequestered into a neat theoretical package. Indeed a picture such as the "flagstone" piece, with its irresistible illusionism and iridescent surface, could be considered to either support or contradict Greenberg's famous observation of the result of Olitski's mid-1960s spray painting: ". . . it contrives an illusion of depth that somehow extrudes all suggestions of depth back to the picture's surface." According to Greenberg these works also contained "a world of light differentiations impossible to flatness but which yet manage not to violate flatness."[3] On the one hand, I wondered what was foremost in Olitski's mind when he made this "flagstone" picture: formal concerns or just the pleasure of painting. Or could these playful, tactile, and illusionist tendencies of this mid-1980s painting already be signs of what *New York Times* art critic Roberta Smith recently intimated as Olitski's postmodern impulse?[4]

Contradictions abound not only within the writings on Jules Olitski but also within his broad-gauged and ambitious art, given his continuously experimental and vigorously experiential means of picture making. Such oppositions are evident already in the dialectical tension of Greenberg's remarks quoted earlier in which the forces of depth's illusion fight against the inviolable laws of flatness. Michael Fried too recognized Olitski's contradictory impulses. He accommodated them to his fine-tuned analysis noting how the mid-1960s paintings with their seeming "indeterminate space" countered the logical, cohesive, "deductive" shapes that ordered the more precisely structured canvases of Olitski's fellow Color Field painters Kenneth Noland and Frank Stella. Fried also recognized Olitski's less rational instincts like "intuition," "passion," "resourcefulness," and "humor"—personal traits that remain distinguishing characteristics of the artist's sensibility, and qualities that permitted the works (as well as the later paintings) to be "contemplated," "enjoyed," and "embraced."[5] A further example of the formalist tautologies mentioned above came from Walter Darby Bannard who noted the seemingly incongruous way Olitski was able to keep his surfaces at once "opaque" and "transparent."[6] And early on Barbara Rose nattily observed how the paint in Olitski's pictures of 1962 seems to have "spontaneously flooded the canvas," the contradiction for her being that the painting seemed to make itself at the same time that Olitski was creating it.[7]

Greenberg's and Fried's were the canonical writings about Olitski and about Color Field painting. Within a relatively short time some critics began to warn of the limitations of formalist criticism in relation to reading his later work, at least they saw it as an encumbrance to the enjoyment of his Apollonian art. As early as 1968, Andrew Hudson already understood Olitski's impulse to go against the grain noting his "delight

. . . at letting things happen in his art that look distasteful . . . his impulses to go against any hand of accepted convention, or tastes."[8] In an extended review for *Art News* devoted to Olitski's 1973 retrospective at the Boston Museum of Fine Arts, Jeanne Siegel tellingly analyzed the problems surrounding the critique on Olitski, at the same time revealing much about Olitski's crucial position in the discussions about American art of that moment.

> Discourses on [the] format [of the artist's spray pictures], along with disputes
> about his success or lack of success in achieving flatness, have made Olitski
> one of the most controversial figures associated with recent formalist art.
> While these arguments are not necessarily invalid, they have obscured what
> really makes the paintings so beautiful to look at.[9]

Another contradiction emerges from Siegel's observations, notably the incongruity between Olitski's "dramatic" effects and his usual association with the "cool" temperament of the art of the 1960s with which he was closely identified.[10] Recently, Karen Wilkin, a critic of formalist lineage and instinct who traces her intellectual formation directly to Clement Greenberg, recognized what she calls "a life after formalism" for the Color Field artists like Helen Frankenthaler, Anthony Caro, Kenneth Noland and of course Jules Olitski. She noted how over the last forty years many explored "a host of other ideas . . . notions diametrically opposed to the issues that engaged them most deeply at the start of their careers." These included but were not limited to "illusionism, reference and even narrative." She playfully refers to these latter directions as "transgressions" from the earlier, abiding formalist regulations.[11]

Of course, Harold Rosenberg, the person who conceived of the idea of "action painting" in contradistinction to Clement Greenberg's formal method, avoided and danced around Olitski. As art critic for *The New Yorker* between 1967 and 1978, he contended with the important presence of Color Field artists on the scene during his tenure. In particular he was disturbed by the writings about them, naturally finding those objective, formalist approaches devoid of the personal, biographical data that were crucial to his subjective, existential method. One of his references to Olitski—albeit somewhat ironic, claimed the artist as an Action painter. Obviously, the Action critic was tantalized by the action potential of Olitski's innovation of spraying paint as well as Olitski's famous metaphor of hoping he could trap paint (without canvas) in pure air. Despite his resistance to admiring Greenberg's favorite artists (Greenberg and Rosenberg did occasionally agree on artists), Rosenberg ultimately succumbed to the beauty of one of Olitski's monumental canvases. He called the artist's *Magic Number* a " . . . most intellectually expressive environment . . . despite its coolness . . . " and

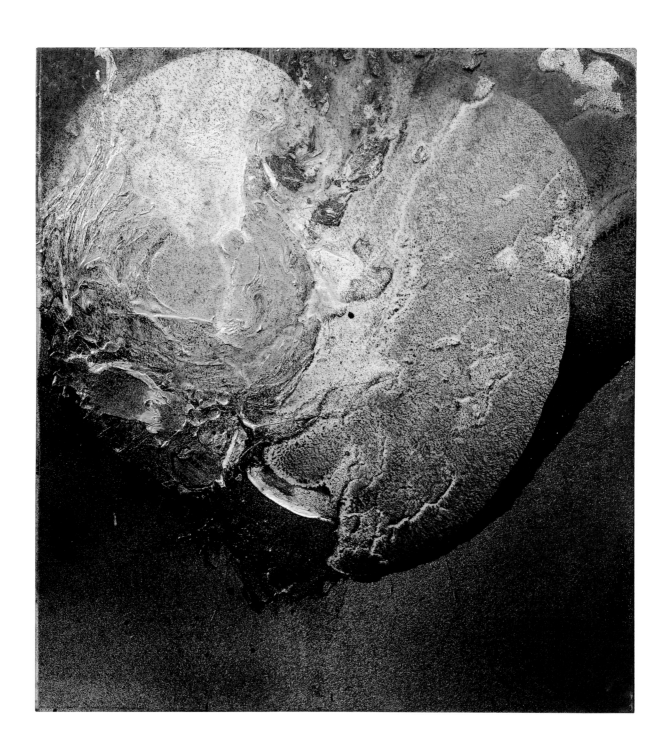

Origins: Patchogue, 2000, acrylic on canvas, 39 x 36 inches

continued to cleverly consider the "quantitative thinking" surrounding Color Field as potentially conducive to magic. Rosenberg simultaneously quoted his colleague and friend Thomas Hess who observed that the light (a very important notion for Rosenberg) in Olitski's *Magic Number* emanated from the interior of the picture, that is the painting glowed.[12]

Olitski's later work is as complex and eclectic as it is elusive and compelling. It refuses to embrace one signature, canonical, easy-to-recognize style which might help define and codify the resulting achievements as either singular vision or marketable product. Oltiski's references are many; his use of them unabashed—from the sensibility of the old masters to the techniques of the moderns. When imagery seeped back into the artist's work in the 1990s it seems clearly a nod to the nineteenth-century Romantic painters where meaning was engendered as much in subject matter as it was in expressive paint manipulation. The mature works, with all their visual and tactile range, must be considered a monumental, synthetic project. They draw from many sources that Olitski internalized, techniques he assimilated, and the beliefs he sustained. No evolutionary grail showed up here, but rather the workings of a confident, deft hand and a facile, far-ranging mind. As with the late "style" of many important artists, there was for Olitski a deep understanding of the past while he clearly resided in the present. To understand his late pictures, we might do well to avoid looking to other critics and writers and return to the thoughts and words of the artist himself. Olitski felt that "play" was essential to the creation of convincing works that reflected the clear voice of the artist. "Imagination, intelligence, intuition, and experience" served as constituents of his clear, unique, yet multifaceted vision. In the mid-1980s, Olitski gladly admitted reintroducing methods and techniques he had previously abandoned probably because they might have been considered too old-masterly, too traditional—even atavistic. Earlier methods such as "under-painting, modeling, half-tones, impasto, chiaroscuro, tinting, and glazing," were deployed by Olitksi into something fresh and new.[13] The range they provide enabled his variety and his syntheses. He constantly combined these traditional practices with newly invented materials that could offer new prospects or fresh versions of older effects.

Among the earliest of the works in this exhibition is a group of modest scale canvases including *Origins: Patchogue*, *Pleasure Whirl: Black*, and *Pleasure Whirl: Yellow*. These were among the first pictures Olitski made after his surgery for lung cancer in 2000—a revelation for a man who thought he would neither survive surgery nor paint again. And after a number of years of painting figurative work with imagery drawn from both biblical texts and the natural world, they were a return to abstraction, but a kind of abstraction forever freighted with imagery. This tension is yet one more contradiction in his practice. The brooding, heavily encrusted works, dense with material, but lean in color, were nearly monochromatic at first. These lunar-like landscapes feel as if they had been pulled directly from a natural geological surface of some far-off planet. Given the title "origins" and the picture's resemblance to a luxurious primordial soup, these works were Olitski's attempt to make his paint reference both artistic creation and natural wonder simultaneously. Like the "flagstone" painting mentioned earlier, the pictures in this exhibit hover between the incongruous tension of illusion and tactility, depth and flatness, representation and abstraction, the natural and the artificial. Even the most monochromatic works present a complex chromatic range. It seems that in these first few pictures from 2000, Olitski was unusually timid in his palette. As he gradually reintroduced color into his pictures, it was as if the color began to emerge from the edges towards each picture's more neutral center.

Color continued to intensify with *Intimations: Five* and *Bathsheba Reverie—Yellow and Black* of 2001. In the former a golden orb hangs to the left in juxtaposition with an irregular blue and white circular form on the right. Olitski intentionally reticulated the paint on each of these rounded forms, revealing white undercoat and creating an intentional crazing of paint, the latter reminiscent of the unintentional effects of 19th century bitumen in the works of any number of masters from Courbet to Ryder. The forms float above a subtly mottled silvery purple and ochre ground that gives the effect of a flickering night sky; the entire composition is enclosed by the framing devices of icing-thick squiggles of cream-colored paint that hark back ever so vaguely to the edge strokes that framed and contained Olitski's classic sprays of the 1960s.

A larger scale work *Prince Patutsky Memoir: Turquoise and Yellow*, 2004, refers in its title to the familial biography that Olitski used on many earlier paintings, and the bright red classic Olitski border is more controlled than that of *Intimations: Five*. But here the colors reach a high-pitched intensity at the center with the bright blue sphere sitting upon a yellow explosion of color, all underscored with three orange brackets. In the upper right hand corner are more modulated forms, at once gaseous and terrestrial. The terrestrial is sandy and crazed in tone augmented with umber and ochre; the gaseous shoots off bright red flame-like eruptions emanating from a mottled irregular globe. As has been commented before about these works, they evoke landscape and skyscape references, even planetary and supernatural ones that denote nature's energy. The intensity of Olitski's colors can feel jarring when each colored area is observed separately. But the artist is a master of unlikely clashes of intense and artificial-looking colors recalling Delacroix. This volatile brushwork can be connected with William Mallord Turner's paintings at his freest and most explosive, even though the latter have a narrower chromatic range. Olitski's daring use of wild, acid, sometimes acrid shades attached to semi-abstract forms has been virtually unknown since Hans Hofmann's late works. Like Hofmann, Olitski was able to use pairings and clusters of garish hues

Intimations: Five, 2001, acrylic on canvas, 16 x 24 inches

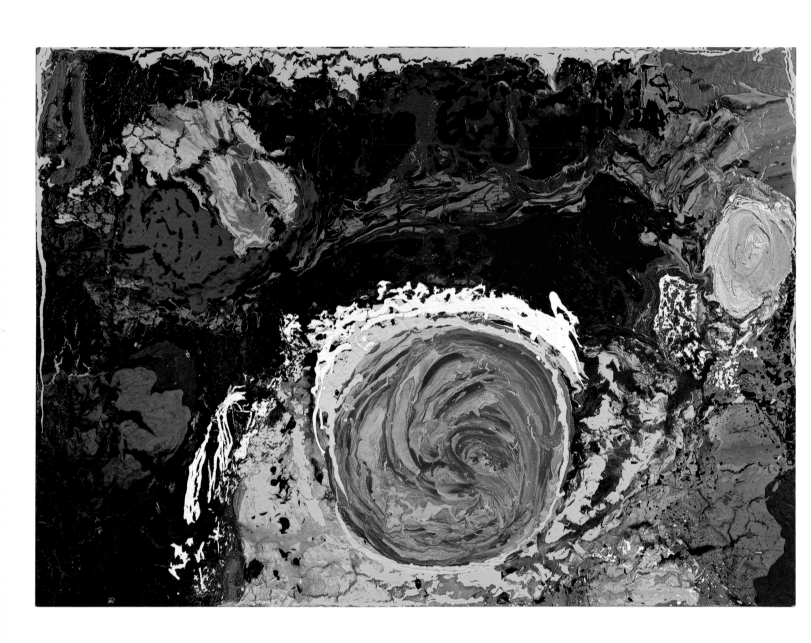

With Love and Disregard: Zeus, 2002, acrylic on canvas, 60 x 84 inches

situated in perfect tension by the "push-pull" of his juxtapositions of form, area, and intensity. Like Hofmann's nearly abstract block pictures, the works always contain references to nature, in Hofmann's case real, in Olitski's imagined. Olitski's painterly effects allude to atmospheric phenomena and the sense of awe for the cosmos about which he spoke so passionately. Works like *Revelation: Yellow, Red and Green* of 2006 are even more intense in effect and chromatic brightness, even through the palette is more limited, with its black outlines both framing and breaking the thickly laid on yellow, white and pinkish forms.

If there could be a summation picture to Olitski's career, it is likely to be *With Love and Disregard: Zeus* of 2002. The large sphere of tensely wound orange and yellow paint in the lower half of the picture spins off a yellow and white painterly blast from its undercoat. There is a tension between the solar reference and the notion that Olitski has set his paint in eternal motion. The usual framing devices, holdovers from 1960s practice, now bleed off the canvas, remaining at once part of the atmospheric chaos and part painterly turmoil. *With Love and Disregard* is a perfect composition of violent imagery, a collision of creation and destruction. Here is a perfect balance of form and color, the playful shapes and textures, and a fusion of natural allusion and painterly reality make this (and so many other Olitskis) what de Kooning once called a living picture. The themes of these paintings evince Olitski's close connection with both nature and ethical humanism. They also evince his belief in a power outside himself and the potential for creativity within each individual. Such sensibilities result from his constant struggle to see with fresh eyes while experimenting and perfecting his craft. There are transcendant aspects to Olitski's last works—and to his entire oeuvre for that matter—that are best summed up in two of his oft-reiterated mantras: "wonder is sacred" and "creation is communion with a divine source."[14]

— Norman L. Kleeblatt

Susan and Elihu Rose Chief Curator, The Jewish Museum, New York

1. Henry Geldzahler, "Interview with Jules Olitski: April 11 and 12, 1990," in Henry Geldzahler, Tim Hilton, Dominique Fourcade, *Jules Olitski*, Exh. cat. (New York: Salander O'Reilly Galleries, 1990), 10.
2. Jules Olitski, "How My Art Gets Made," *Partisan Review* (Fall 2001), 618.
3. Clement Greenberg, *The Collected Essays and Criticism*, vol. 4, Modernism with a Vengeance, 1957–1969. John O'Brien, ed. (Chicago and London, The University of Chicago Press, 1993), 229.
4. Roberta Smith, "Art in Review: Jules Olitski," *The New York Times* (October 14, 2005), E36.
5. Michael Fried, "Jules Olitski's New Paintings," *Artforum* (November 1965), 36–40.
6. Walter Darby Bannard, "Notes on American Painting of the Sixties," *Artforum* (January 1970), 45.
7. Barbara Rose, "New York Letter," *Art International* 7 (April 1964), 57.
8. Andrew Hudson, "On Jules Olitski's Paintings—And Some Changes of View," *Art International* XII, no. 1 (January 1968), 31.
9. Jeanne Siegel, "Olitski's retrospective: infinite variety," *Art News* (Summer 1973), 61.
10. Ibid., 63.
11. Karen Wilkin, "Life After Formalism," *Art in America* (November 2001), 111.
12. Harold Rosenberg, "Big," *Artworks & Packages* (Chicago: University of Chicago Press, 1982), 122. Olitski fondly remembered Rosenberg's flattering mention of *Magic Number*. Interview with the artist January 2007.
13. Jules Olitski, [not titled] in Phillip L. Berman, ed. *The Courage of Conviction* (New York: The Center for the Study of Belief, Dodd, Mead and Co. 1985), 189.
14. Ibid., 185, 192.

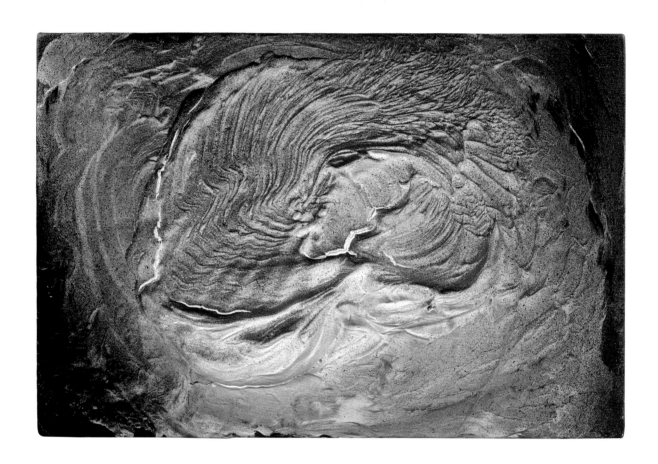

Pleasure Whirl: Yellow, 2000, acrylic on canvas, 16 x 24 inches

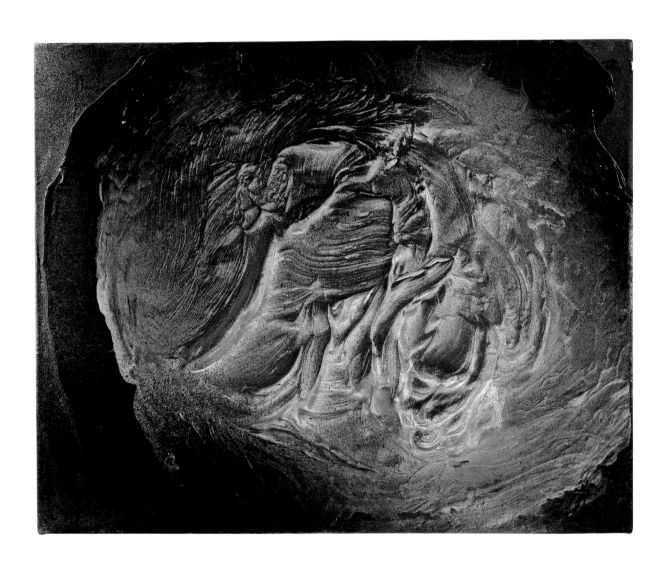

Pleasure Whirl: Black, 2000, acrylic on canvas, 24 x 30 inches

Bathsheba Reverie—Yellow and Black, 2001, acrylic on canvas, 30 x 40 inches

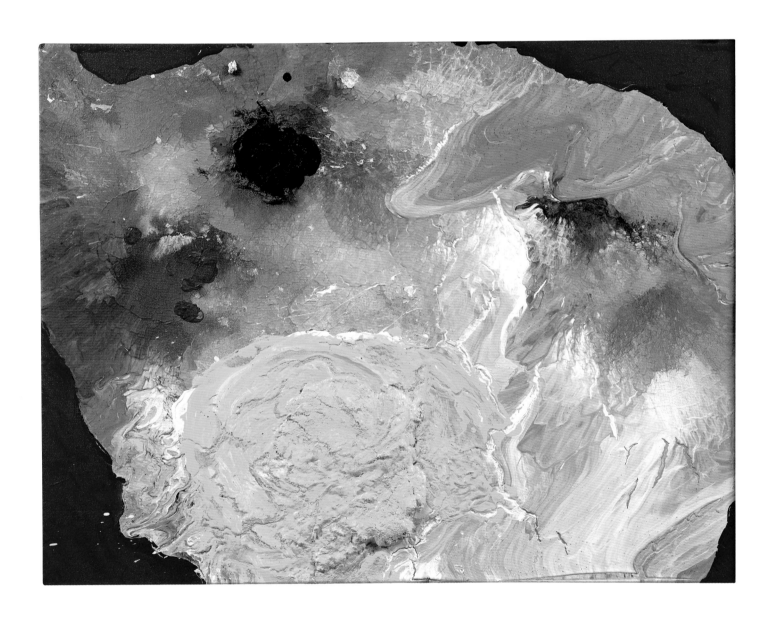

Moses Path—Lavender and Green, 2001, acrylic on canvas, 48 x 40 inches

Bathsheba Reverie—Violet, 2001, acrylic on canvas, 20 x 16 inches

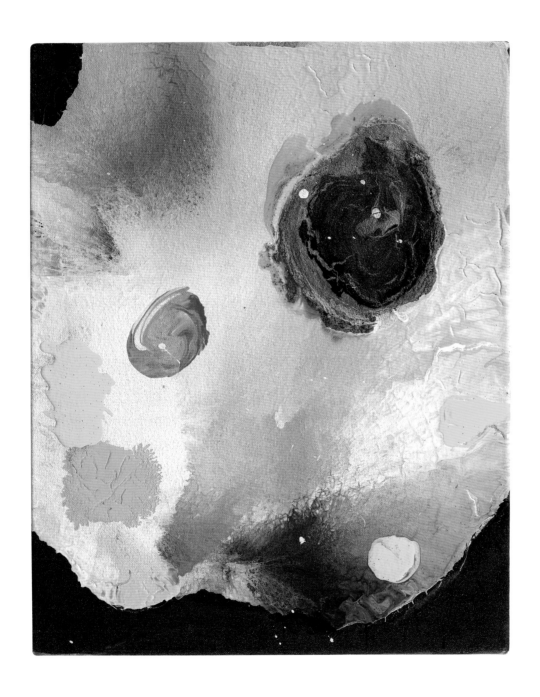

Temptation: Yellow, 2002, acrylic on canvas, 60 x 72 inches

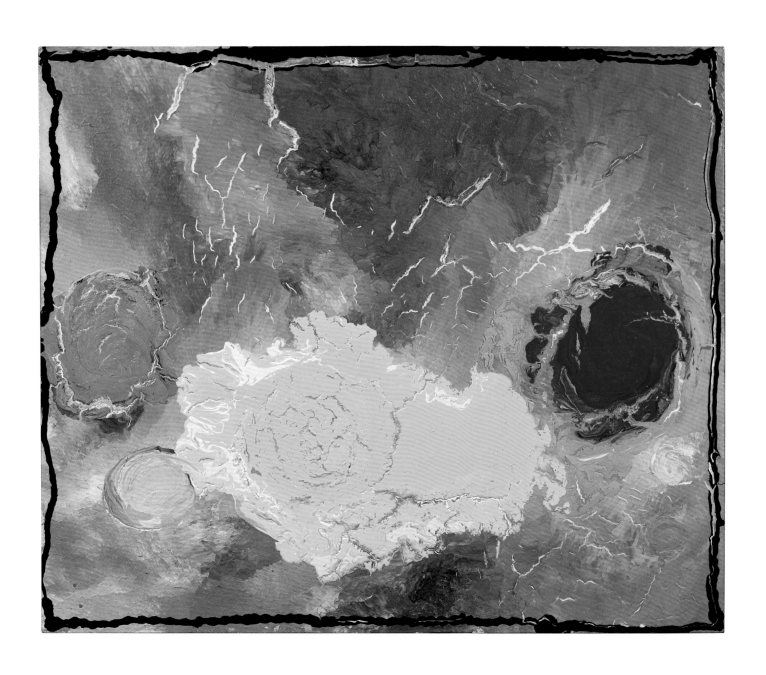

With Love and Disregard: Journey of Solomon, 2002, acrylic on canvas, 36 x 48 inches

Memoirs: Yellow and White, 2003, acrylic on canvas, 30 x 35 inches

By Love Unlocked: Beauty, 2003, acrylic on canvas, 60 x 72 inches

Wanderings: Seville, Orange and Blue, 2004, acrylic on canvas, 16 x 20 inches

Wanderings: Toledo, Yellow and Green, 2004, acrylic on canvas, 16 x 20 inches

Wanderings: Bilbao, Yellow and Black, 2004, acrylic on canvas, 20 x 16 inches

Embraced: Rose and Black, 2005, acrylic on canvas, 40 1/2 x 29 1/2 inches

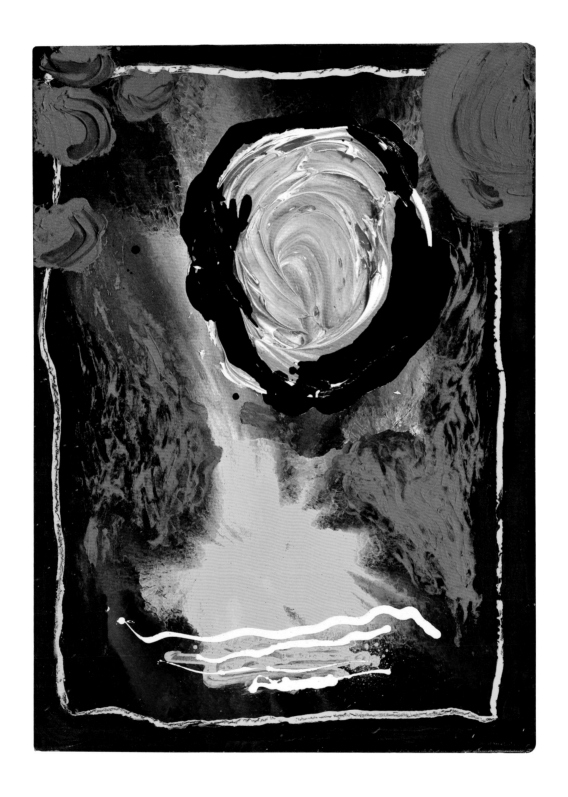

Patutsky Embraced: Orange and Green, 2005, acrylic on canvas, 48 x 40 inches

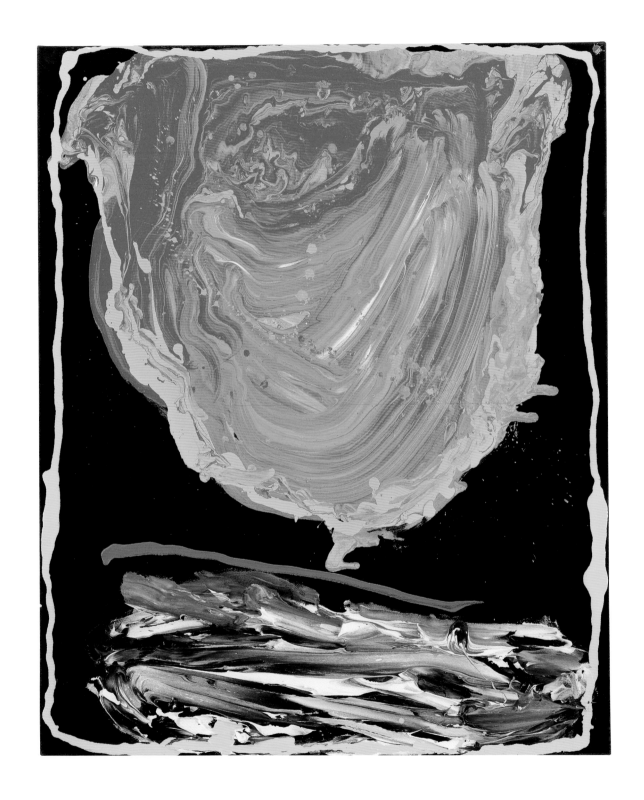

Revelation: Red, Black and Turquoise, 2006, acrylic on canvas, 34 x 36 inches

Revelation: Yellow, Red and Green, 2006, acrylic on canvas, 18 1/2 x 23 inches

Revelation: Yellow, Orange and Green, 2006, acrylic on canvas, 20 x 20 inches

The Sixth Visit, 2006, acrylic on canvas, 40 x 48 inches

Celebrate: Red, 2007, acrylic on canvas, 9 x 12 inches

50   Jules Olitski in his New Hampshire studio, 1996. Photograph by Helen Miljakovich

JULES OLITSKI (1922–2007)

Jules Olitski was born in Russia in 1922, a few months before his father was executed by the Soviet government. His mother and grandmother soon emigrated with him to the U.S., settling in Brooklyn. Olitski eventually studied art at the National Academy School of Fine Arts and the Beaux-Arts Institute, and he earned an M.A. from New York University. Olitski had his first solo exhibition at Galerie Huit in Paris in 1951, and his first New York show in 1959 at French & Company. In 1966, he was one of four artists (with Helen Frankenthaler, Roy Lichtenstein, and Ellsworth Kelly) selected by Henry Geldzahler to represent the U.S. in the 33rd Venice Biennale. In 1969, he was the first living American artist to be given a solo exhibition at The Metropolitan Museum of Art.

Jules Olitski was awarded the Milton and Sally Avery Distinguished Professorship, Bard College, in 1987. He was a Fellow of the American Academy of Arts and Sciences (1991) and a member of the American Academy of Arts and Letters (2006). He was presented with honorary doctorates by the University of Hartford (1997), Keene State College (1998) and Southern New Hampshire University (2003).

Jules Olitski continued to paint and exhibit until his recent death, at age 84, in February 2007. In Spring 2007 he was posthumously awarded the Skowhegan Medal for Painting.

Selected Solo Exhibitions: The Luther W. Brady Art Gallery, The George Washington University, Washington, D.C. (2006); The Goldman Warehouse, Miami, Florida (2005); The McInnch Art Gallery, Southern New Hampshire University, Manchester (2003); Portland Museum of Art, Maine (1998); The Butler Institute of American Art, Youngstown, Ohio (1997); Thorne-Sagendorph Gallery, Keene State College, New Hampshire (1993, 1996, 1999, 2003); David Winton Bell Gallery, List Art Center, Brown University, Providence, Rhode Island (1992); Fondation du Château de Jau, Perpignan, France (1984); Edmonton Art Gallery, Alberta, Canada (1979); Knoedler & Company, New York (1973/87, 2005/07); Museum of Fine Arts, Boston, Massachusetts (1973, 1977); The University of Michigan Museum of Art, Ann Arbor (1971); The Metropolitan Museum of Art, New York (1969); Institute of Contemporary Art, University of Pennsylvania, Philadelphia (1968); The Corcoran Gallery of Art, Washington, D.C. (1967, 1974); André Emmerich Gallery, New York (1966/68, 1978/96); David Mirvish Gallery, Toronto, Ontario, Canada (1964/74); Bennington College, Vermont (1962); French & Company, New York (1959/61); Galerie Huit, Paris (1951).

Selected Group Exhibitions: *The Abstract Impulse: Fifty Years of Abstraction at the National Academy, 1956–2006,* National Academy Museum, New York (2007); *Clement Greenberg: A Critic's Collection,* Portland Art Museum, Oregon (2001); *After Matisse,* Independent Curators Incorporated (traveling exhibition, 1986–88); *New York Painting and Sculpture, 1940–1970,* The Metropolitan Museum of Art, New York (1970); *Three American Painters: Kenneth Noland, Jules Olitski, Frank Stella,* Fogg Art Museum, Harvard University Art Museums, Cambridge, Massachusetts (1965); *Three New American Painters: Louis, Noland, Olitski,* MacKenzie Art Gallery, University of Regina, Saskatchewan, Canada (1963); *Whitney Annual Exhibition of Contemporary American Painting,* New York (1962, 1967, 1968, 1969, 1972, 1973).

Public Collections: Albright-Knox Art Gallery, Buffalo, New York; Art Gallery of Ontario, Toronto, Canada; The Art Institute of Chicago, Illinois; David Winton Bell Gallery, List Art Center, Brown University, Providence, Rhode Island; Brooklyn Museum, New York; Cincinnati Art Museum, Ohio; The Corcoran Gallery of Art, Washington, D.C.; Cranbrook Art Museum, Bloomfield Hills, Michigan; Dallas Museum of Art, Texas; Davis Museum and Cultural Center, Wellesley College, Massachusetts; The Detroit Institute of Arts, Michigan; Edmonton Art Gallery, Alberta, Canada; Fogg Art Museum, Harvard University Art Museums, Cambridge, Massachusetts; Solomon R. Guggenheim Museum, New York; Hirshhorn Museum and Sculpture Garden, Washington, D.C.; The Israel Museum, Jerusalem; The Joseloff Gallery/Hartford Art School, West Hartford, Connecticut; Krannert Art Museum, University of Illinois at Urbana-Champaign; Kunstsammlung Nordrhein-Westfalen, Düsseldorf, Germany; The Metropolitan Museum of Art, New York; Milwaukee Art Museum, Wisconsin; MIT-List Visual Arts Center, Cambridge, Massachusetts; Musée d'Art Contemporain de Lyon, France; Musée d'Art Moderne et d'Art Contemporain, Nice, France; Musée National du Château de Jau, Perpignan, France; Museum Moderner Kunst, Stiftung Ludwig, Vienna, Austria; Museum of Contemporary Art, Los Angeles, California; Museum of Contemporary Art, Miami, Florida; Museum of Contemporary Art, Sydney, Australia; Museum of Fine Arts, Boston, Massachusetts; The Museum of Fine Arts, Houston, Texas; The Museum of Modern Art, New York; National Academy Museum, New York; National Gallery of Art, Washington, D.C.; National Gallery of Australia, Canberra; National Gallery of Canada, Ottawa, Ontario; The Nelson-Atkins Museum of Art, Kansas City, Missouri; Neuberger Museum of Art, Purchase College, State University of New York; Pennsylvania Academy of the Fine Arts, Philadelphia; Portland Art Museum, Oregon; Princeton University Art Museum, New Jersey; Rose Art Museum, Brandeis University, Waltham, Massachusetts;

San Francisco Museum of Modern Art, California; Seattle Art Museum, Washington; Smith College Museum of Art, Northampton, Massachusetts; Smithsonian American Art Museum, Washington, D.C.; Storm King Art Center, Mountainville, New York; Tate Modern, London, England; Tel Aviv Museum of Art, Israel; Thorne-Sagendorph Art Gallery, Keene State College, New Hampshire; The University of Michigan Museum of Art, Ann Arbor; Wadsworth Atheneum, Hartford, Connecticut; Walker Art Center, Minneapolis, Minnesota; Whitney Museum of American Art, New York; Yale University Art Gallery, New Haven, Connecticut.

Writings on the Artist: Carl Belz, *Jules Olitski—Matter Embraced: Paintings 1950s and Now* (2005); John Elderfield, "Painterliness Redefined: Jules Olitski and Recent Abstract Art," Parts I and II, *Art International* (December 1972, April 1973); Terry Fenton, *Jules Olitski and the Tradition of Oil Painting* (1979); Michael Fried, "Art and Objecthood," *Artforum* (Summer 1967) and "Fields of Vision," *Artforum* (April 2007); Henry Geldzahler, Tim Hilton, and Dominique Fourcade, *Jules Olitski* (1990); Norman L. Kleeblatt, *Jules Olitski: The Late Paintings—A Celebration* (2007); Kenworth Moffett, *Jules Olitski* (1981); Lauren Poster, editor, with Jules Olitski, Jim Walsh, John Walters, et al., *Jules Olitski: The New Hampshire Exhibits* (2004); Jules Olitski, "Jules Olitski on Himself," in *Modern Painters: Writers on Artists* (2001); Karen Wilkin, *Jules Olitski: Six Decades* (2005).

With our heartfelt thanks to Jules Olitski's devoted family
for making possible this exhibition celebrating his late work.

Special thanks to Kristina Olitski, and Lauren and Bradley Poster.

Published on the occasion of the exhibition

JULES OLITSKI
THE LATE PAINTINGS
A CELEBRATION

November 8, 2007–January 5, 2008

Knoedler & Company
19 East 70 Street New York New York 10021
Tel 212 794-0550 Fax 212 772-6932
www.knoedlergallery.com

Color transparencies by Jeff Baird, Brattleboro, Vermont

Catalogue designed by The Grenfell Press, New York

Printed by Trifolio, Verona, Italy

Cover: detail *Bathsheba Reverie—Yellow and Black,* 2001,
acrylic on canvas, 30 x 40 inches

"A Culmination of Contradictions: Jules Olitski's Last Decade"
Copyright © 2007 Norman L. Kleeblatt

Publication copyright © 2007 Knoedler & Company

ISBN: 0-9789987-5-8